Germain

Hello, Family Members,

Learning to read is one [of the] [importa]nt accomplishments of early childhoo[d. These books ar]e designed to help children become [readers who love t]o read. Beginning readers learn [to read by rememberin]g frequently used words like "the," ["and," and "is"; b]y using phonics skills to decode new words; [and by] interpreting picture and text clues. These books provide both the stories children enjoy and the structure they need to read fluently and independently. Here are suggestions for helping your child *before*, *during*, and *after* reading:

Before

- Look at the cover and pictures and have your child predict what the story is about.
- Read the story to your child.
- Encourage your child to chime in with familiar words and phrases.
- Echo read with your child by reading a line first and having your child read it after you do.

During

- Have your child think about a word he or she does not recognize right away. Provide hints such as "Let's see if we know the sounds" and "Have we read other words like this one?"
- Encourage your child to use phonics skills to sound out new words.
- Provide the word for your child when more assistance is needed so that he or she does not struggle and the experience of reading with you is a positive one.
- Encourage your child to have fun by reading with a lot of expression . . . like an actor!

After

- Have your child keep lists of interesting and favorite words.
- Encourage your child to read the books over and over again. Have him or her read to brothers, sisters, grandparents, and even teddy bears. Repeated readings develop confidence in young readers.
- Talk about the stories. Ask and answer questions. Share ideas about the funniest and most interesting characters and events in the stories.

I do hope that you and your child enjoy this book.

—Francie Alexander
　Reading Specialist,
　Scholastic's Learning Ventures

To my mother, Mildred Jones,
and my sister, Vanessa
—L.J.

For Ann D'Amico
—D.B.

Text copyright © 1999 by Lynda Jones.
Illustrations copyright © 1999 by Don Bolognese.
All rights reserved. Published by Scholastic Inc.
SCHOLASTIC, HELLO READER! and CARTWHEEL BOOKS and associated logos are trademarks and/or registered trademarks of Scholastic Inc.

Library of Congress Cataloging-in-Publication Data

Jones, Lynda.
    Abe Lincoln / by Lynda Jones; illustrated by Don Bolognese.
        p.   cm.— (Hello reader! Level 4)
    "Cartwheel books."
    Summary: Follows the life of one of the best known presidents of the United States, from his birth in Kentucky to his assassination at the end of the Civil War.
    ISBN 0-590-87581-7
    1.Lincoln, Abraham, 1809-1865 — Juvenile literature.
    2.Presidents — United States — Biography — Juvenile literature
    [1. Lincoln, Abraham, 1809-1865. 2. Presidents.] I. Bolognese, Don, ill.
    II. Title. III. Series.
    E457.905.J661999
    973.7'092— dc21   98-22744
    [B]   CIP
                                                                                     AC
12 11 10 9 8 7 6 5 4 3 2 1   9/9 0/0 01 02 03 04

Printed in the U.S.A.   24
First printing, February 1999

Abe Lincoln

by Lynda Jones
Illustrated by Don Bolognese

Hello Reader! — Level 4

SCHOLASTIC INC.
New York   Toronto   London   Auckland   Sydney

Chapter 1
A Busy Boy

Cold winter winds whistled outside a one-room log cabin on a farm in Hardin County, Kentucky. Inside, a newborn baby boy cried and cried. He lay on a bed made of bearskin and cornhusks. It was February 12, 1809. Thomas and Nancy Hanks Lincoln smiled at their son. "We'll name him Abraham," they said to little Sarah, their two-year-old. Everyone would call the boy Abe.

Baby Abe's nine-year-old cousin Dennis Hanks couldn't wait to see him. Dennis raced through the woods to the cabin. He stared at Abe's wrinkled red face. *Why, he looks like a squeezed cherry*, thought Dennis.

"Can I hold him?" he asked.

Nancy gently handed him the baby. "Be careful, Dennis," she said softly.

Dennis held the baby close in his arms. Little Abe cried and cried. "Aunt, take him!" Dennis said, all annoyed. "He'll never come to much."

But Dennis was wrong.

Young Abe grew strong and healthy. He liked to wear buckskin pants and a coonskin hat. He often went on raccoon hunts with his Pappy. A curious child, Abe would even follow bees to their hives. And he loved to fish in a nearby creek.

One day, Abe and a friend were playing at the creek. Suddenly there was a big SPLASH! Abe had slipped and fallen into the creek — and he couldn't get out! He almost drowned. But his friend grabbed a long tree branch and fished Abe out of the water. Abe was very lucky.

Although he loved to have fun, young Abe worked hard on the farm, too. The Lincolns were very poor. They made their own clothes. For food, they hunted and grew vegetables. Abe helped out a lot. He gathered firewood and berries and nuts. He fetched water. And he tried to help plant vegetables, too. But Abe's planting didn't always turn out the way he had hoped.

On a bright Saturday morning, Abe planted a handful of pumpkin seeds. *How big will my pumpkins grow?* he wondered. Poor Abe never found out. On Sunday morning heavy rains poured down. The flood of rainwater washed over the soil and swept the seeds clear off the land!

Abe went to school when he was six years old. The one-room schoolhouse was miles away from home. Abe and his older sister, Sarah, walked through the snowy forest to get there. Abe's moccasins got so wet that his feet were frozen cold. And it was so cold inside that Abe's fingers felt frozen, too. Sitting on the rough, hard bench didn't help Abe feel any better either.

When he first walked into the classroom, Abe thought, *What a lot of noise!* All the children said their lessons out loud until they knew them by heart. Everyone talked at the same time. But Abe got used to the noise, of course, when he joined in.

Abe learned his A, B, C's and 1, 2, 3's. He learned to write his name. He practiced spelling by writing words in the dirt with a stick. He became the best speller in the school. Abe wrote poetry, too. And he wrote letters for neighbors who couldn't read or write.

Abe didn't go to school when his father needed him on the farm. Abe's schooling added up to less than a year. But that didn't stop Abe from learning. He read everything he could. "A friend is someone who finds me a new book to read," he later said.

Chapter 2
A New Home for Abe

One day, Abe's Pappy said to the family, "It's time to move." He said they would be moving to Little Pigeon Creek, Indiana. *What will Indiana be like?* Abe wondered. He helped his family pile their belongings onto two horses. And they were off to a new home.

It was a long trip. Abe rode. Then he walked.
Finally the Lincolns boarded a flatboat. They
traveled for miles on the Ohio River. It was
winter. The water was cold. The bitter wind chilled
Abe to the bone.

The land in Indiana was wild. Abe's eyes grew wide as they walked through the dark woods. *I hope no wild animals attack!* Abe thought.

The family had no home in Indiana. Building a new log cabin would take a long time. In the meantime, Abe helped to build a three-sided shelter. It was made of logs, mud, and branches. On the open

side, Abe started a fire to keep everyone warm day and night.

Abe slept on the ground. He made a bed of dry leaves and bearskins. He listened to the wolves howl. He listened to the panthers roar. Abe shook with fear.

Life in Indiana got even harder for Abe. When he was nine, his mother died from a disease called "milk sickness." Abe was so, so sad. He felt all alone. "What will I do without my Mammy?" he cried.

One day a year later, Abe's Pappy came home smiling. With him, in the wagon was a rosy-cheeked woman. "This is your new Mammy," said Pappy. Her name was Sarah Bush Johnston. She had three children. Now four more people lived in the Lincoln's one-room cabin. It was not cozy. But Abe loved his stepmother. She encouraged him to read.

Chapter 3
Abe Grows Up

Abe grew tall, then taller. He spent his days clearing the land for farming. He chopped trees with his axe. He split logs to make fences. "My, how he can chop!" said the neighbors. They wanted Abe to work for them, too. His Pappy said okay.

All that chopping made Abe strong. But Abe hated farm work. He wanted to use his mind, not his muscles. "My father taught me to work," said Abe, "but he never taught me to love it."

Sometimes Abe was shy. Sometimes he wasn't. He told many jokes and funny stories. He stood on a tree stump and imitated people. Everyone laughed and laughed. When Abe wasn't goofing off, he was

reading. He would read and plow the fields at the same time. Some thought Abe was strange for reading so much. Others thought Abe was just plain lazy.

By the time Abe was sixteen, he was six feet tall. His pants were too short for his long, skinny legs. His hair was always messy. He had big, bony hands and large feet. People made fun of his weird looks. But Abe's strong, lean body helped him become a good wrestler and a fast runner.

Although he had many things to keep him busy, Abe grew tired of the frontier life. At seventeen, he left home to become a ferryman. He worked on a ferryboat that took travelers across the Ohio River to big steamboats.

Abe was excited to have this job. He was happy to earn his own money. He never forgot the day two travelers paid him two shiny half dollars. That was a *lot* of money then. Abe couldn't believe his good luck. "I, a poor boy, had earned a dollar in less than a day!" he said. But he wasn't rich for long. Clumsy Abe dropped one of the coins in the river.

When he was nineteen, Abe got a job where he would take a much longer trip. He was hired to go to New Orleans with a store-owner's son. They were to sell farm products there. Abe was thrilled. He was going to a big city for the first time.

The young men built a flatboat to take them down the Mississippi River. On the river, Abe rowed day and night. He rowed through sun, fog, and rain. The waters were rough, but Abe was strong.

One night, the young men stopped to rest. A gang of thieves attacked them. The thieves tried to rob them. But Abe was big. He was six feet four inches tall. Abe grabbed a hickory club and fought the men. He chased them away. But a punch from one of the thieves wounded Abe over his right eye. For the rest of his life, Abe had a scar over that eyebrow. And he never forgot that scary night.

When they got to New Orleans, Abe and his friend saw many people. They saw sailors and boats from all over the world. They heard people speaking strange languages. They saw busy shops and buildings. Abe's excitement grew. But it soon disappeared.

Abe saw Black men, women, and children chained like animals. They were slaves. Slaves worked hard in the plantation fields from sunup to sundown. They did not get paid for the work they did. Abe thought this was wrong. He wished he could do something to help them.

Chapter 4
Abe on His Own

When he was twenty-one years old, Abe moved to New Salem, Illinois. He worked as a shopkeeper, a postmaster, a mapmaker and at other jobs. Finally, Abe decided to become a lawyer. He wanted to help people. He studied hard for three years.

Abe opened a law office in Springfield, Illinois. He was a smart and honest lawyer. People called him "Honest Abe." But Abe was forgetful. He often forgot where he put important papers and letters. Then he had an idea of a safe place to keep them. He would stuff the papers inside his black high hat!

One winter evening, Abe went to a dance. There, he met a young woman named Mary Todd. They fell in love. On November 4, 1842, Abe and Mary were married. Abe and Mary had four sons: Robert, Edward, William, and Thomas. The boys often visited Abe at his law office. What a noise they all made in the office, father and sons playing together!

As a lawyer, Abe helped many people. But he wanted to do more. He worked as a congressman and a senator, making laws for people. Then on November 6, 1860, Abe got his biggest job of all. He was elected the 16th president of the United States of America. There were parades and fireworks. He was so proud! No one ever guessed that a poor country boy would become such an important man.

President Lincoln and his family moved into the White House. He had a lot of work to do. A war started between the Northern states and the Southern states. The South wanted slavery to continue. The North didn't. Many soldiers fought and died. This made Abe very sad. He wanted to end the war. He wanted to free the slaves.

On September 22, 1862, President Lincoln presented an important paper, the Emancipation Proclamation. This paper helped free many slaves in the South. Three years later, a new law freed slaves everywhere in the United States — forever. Although slavery was over, the war went on.

In November 1864, Abe Lincoln was elected president for a second time! Many people came to the White House to congratulate Abe. An ex-slave, Frederick Douglass, came too. The president shook his hand. "Welcome," said Abe. He was the first president to entertain a Black person in the White House.

A few months after his re-election, on April 9, 1865, President Lincoln received great news. The war was finally over! There were more celebrations all over the country.

Days later, the happy president and his wife went to see a play at Ford's Theater. During the play, an angry man shot the president! The man was an actor named John Wilkes Booth. He was angry that the North had won the war.

The next morning, April 15, 1865, President Abe Lincoln died. A train carried him back to his hometown, Springfield, Illinois. Thousands of people waved good-bye as the train passed. Silently, they thanked Abe for all the wonderful things he had done.

The Lincoln Memorial in Washington, D.C. honors the popular president.